Incredible Mammals

EXPRESS EDITION

John Townsend

www.raintreepublishers.co.uk

Visit our website to find out more information about **Raintree** books.

To order:
☎ Phone 44 (0) 1865 888113
🖹 Send a fax to 44 (0) 1865 314091
💻 Visit the Raintree Bookshop at **www.raintreepublishers.co.uk** to browse our catalogue and order online.

First published in Great Britain by Raintree Publishers,
Halley Court, Jordan Hill, Oxford, OX2 8EJ,
part of Harcourt Education Ltd.
Raintree is a registered trademark of Harcourt
Education Ltd.

© Harcourt Education Ltd 2005
First published in paperback in 2005.

Produced for Raintree Publishers by Discovery Books Ltd
Editorial: Louise Galpine, Elisabeth Taylor,
Charlotte Guillain, and Diyan Leake
Expert Reader: Jill Bailey
Design: Victoria Bevan, Keith Williams (sprout.uk.com
Limited), and Michelle Lisseter
Picture Research: Maria Joannou
Production: Duncan Gilbert and Jonathan Smith
Printed and bound in China by South China
Printing Company
Originated by Repro Multi Warna

ISBN 1 844 43476 1 (hardback)
09 08 07 06 05
10 9 8 7 6 5 4 3 2 1

ISBN 1 844 43584 9 (paperback)
09 08 07 06 05
10 9 8 7 6 5 4 3 2 1

British Library Cataloguing in Publication Data
Townsend, John
Incredible mammals. – (Freestyle express. Incredible creatures)
599
A full catalogue record for this book is available from the British Library.

This levelled text is a version of Freestyle:
Incredible creatures: Incredible mammals.

Photo acknowledgements
The publisher would like to thank the following for permission to reproduce photographs: Alamy Images pp. **20–1**; Ardea p. **10** left (Brian Bevan); FLPA pp. **5** bottom (Terry Whittaker), **6** (Minden Pictures), **7** (Helen Rhode), **16–17** (Foto Natura Stock), **22–3** (Panda Photo), **26–7** (Tony Wharton), **30–1** (Winfried Wisniewski), **34–5** (Gerard Lacz), **38–9** (Minden Pictures), **40–1** (F. W. Lane), **48–9** (Gerard Laoz), **42** left (Terry Whittaker), **42–3** (Minden Pictures), **43** right (P & J Wegner/Foto Natura), **49** (Terry Whittaker); Mike Johnson p. **34**; Naturepl pp. **4** (Anup Shah), **8–9** (Dave Watts), **15** (Martha Holmes), **18–19** (Sharon Heald), **27** (Barry Mansell), **36**, **38** (Pete Oxford); NHPA pp. **5** left (Daniel Heuclin), **5** top (Andy Rouse), **5** middle (Andy Rouse), **6–7** (James Warwick), **8** (Martin Harvey), **9** (Nick Garbutt), **10** right (Stephen Dalton), **11** (Nick Garbutt), **12–13** (Andy Rouse), **13** (John Shaw), **14** left (David E. Meyers), **14** right (Andy Rouse), **16** (T. Kitchin & V. Hurst), **17** (Adrian Hepworth), **19** (Stephen Dalton), **21** (Martin Harvey), **23** (Dave Watts), **24** (Daniel Heuclin), **24–5** (Kevin Schafer), **25** right (Daryl Balfour), **28** left (Martin Harvey), **28–9** (Daryl Balfour), **29** right (Iain Green), **32** left (Jonathan & Angela Scott), **32–3** (Ant Photo Library), **33** right (Paal Hermansen), **35** (Laurie Campbell), **37** top (Andy Rouse), **39** (B & C Alexander), **44** left (Dave Watts), **44–5** (Dave Watts), **46–7** (Martin Harvey), **47** right (John Shaw), **48** (Dave Watts), **50** left (James Carmichael Jr), **50–1** Martin Harvey), **51** right (Ann & Steve Toon); Oxford Scientific Films p. **31** (Mark Hamblin); Photodisc pp. **12**, **20**, **46**; Science Photo Library pp. **26** (Merlin Tuttle/Bat Conservation International), **30**, **41** (Dolphin Institute), **45** (Art Wolfe); The Gorilla Foundation p. **40** (Ron Cohn/kk.org).
Cover photograph of a silverback mountain gorilla reproduced with permission of FLPA (Gerard Lacz)

The Publishers would like to thank Jon Pearce for his assistance in the preparation of this book. Every effort has been made to contact copyright holders of any material reproduced in this book. Any omissions will be rectified in subsequent printings if notice is given to the Publishers.

Contents

Any words appearing in the text in bold, **like this**, are explained in the Glossary. You can also look out for some of them in the 'Wild words' bank at the bottom of each page.

The world of mammals

Can you guess what these are?

- The largest mammal weighs over 130 tonnes – as much as a jumbo jet. Fifty people could stand on its tongue.

- The tallest mammal can be 6 metres – as tall as a double decker bus.

- The fastest mammal can run at 97 kilometres (60 miles) per hour.

Answers are on page 53.

Mammals are the most advanced form of life on Earth. Many of them show high intelligence and amazing skills. They can live in all kinds of places.

There are only just over 4,000 different types or **species** of mammal. One of them has had more impact on the planet than all other animals. That is the human mammal – you and me.

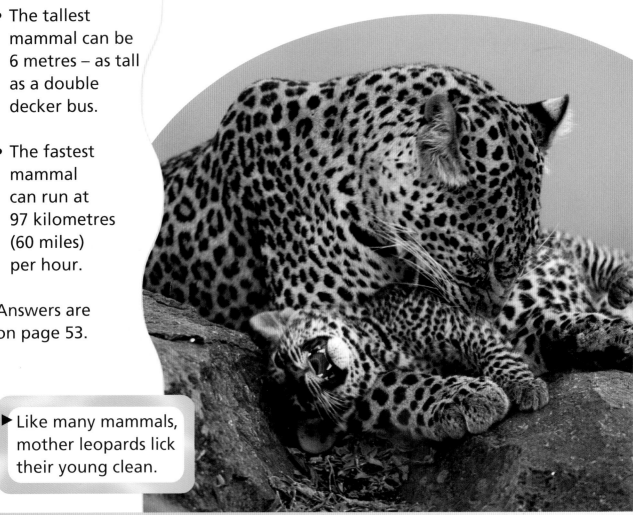

▶ Like many mammals, mother leopards lick their young clean.

species type of animal or plant

What are mammals?

All mammals are **vertebrates**. This means they have backbones. They are warm-blooded. This means they can keep their temperature the same in all weathers. Most mammals give birth to live young, but a few lay eggs.

Female mammals are able to do something that no other creatures can do. They can make milk to feed their young.

Find out later...

... which mammals live in families and look after each other.

Group	Examples
Nibblers and burrowers	rats, mice, and rabbits
Pouched mammals	kangaroos and koalas
Primates	monkeys, apes, and humans
Flying mammals	bats
Insect-eaters	moles and hedgehogs
Grass-eaters	cows, deer, and rhinos
Meat-eaters	lions and wolves
Sea mammals	whales, dolphins, and seals

...which mammal defends itself with a revolting trick.

▲ The pygmy shrew is the smallest mammal.

... which mammals might not be around much longer.

vertebrate animal that has a backbone

Meet the family

Rodents

Imagine an animal that looks a bit like a guinea pig, but is as big as a large dog. That is the South American capybara, the largest **rodent** in the world.

Rodents have sharp front teeth for **gnawing** hard nuts, seeds, and plants. Rats, squirrels, guinea pigs, chipmunks, beavers, and porcupines are just a few of the many different **species** of rodent.

Long life

Porcupines (see below) have been known to live for 27 years. This makes them the longest-living rodents.

rodent mammal with gnawing teeth that keep on growing throughout its life

Rabbits

Rabbits and hares also have large, gnawing teeth. But rabbits and hares have hair on the soles of their feet, unlike rodents.

Members of the rabbit family all have long ears, so they hear well. Their long ears also help to keep them cool. Hares have longer legs than rabbits. They can run over 64 kilometres (40 miles) an hour to escape **predators**.

Making hay

A pika (below) collects grass in the summer. When winter comes, it has hay to eat. Pikas belong to the rabbit family. They are found in the Middle East, Asia, and North America.

▲ The capybara is an excellent swimmer and diver.

Can you believe it?

There were no rabbits in Australia until 24 were taken there in 1859. Ten years later, there were 10 million rabbits!

predator animal that kills and eats other animals

Pouches

Some mammals, called **marsupials**, carry their young around in **pouches** on their bodies. The tiny baby climbs into the pouch as soon as it is born. It grows slowly in there for months, feeding on its mother's milk.

Koalas, kangaroos, possums, and wombats are all marsupials. Most marsupials live in Australia. The Tasmanian devil is as small as a cat but it looks more like a little bear. It can be fierce.

► Young Tasmanian devils make horrible, screeching noises.

Smart mammals

Primates have larger brains for the size of their bodies than other mammals. They also have hands that can grasp, and their eyes are at the front of their heads. This brainy group includes bush babies and lemurs, as well as monkeys, apes, and humans.

Apes, such as chimpanzees and gorillas, are the smartest primates. One primate is far more intelligent than all the others – the human.

Person of the forest

Orang-utan means 'person of the forest'. These intelligent apes live in the rainforests of Borneo. They are in danger of becoming **extinct** because the **rainforest** is being cut down.

primate animal that has a large brain, thumbs, and eyes at the front of its head   9

Smallest bat

The smallest bat in the world is Kitti's hog-nosed bat, also called the bumblebee bat. It is just 3 centimetres (about an inch) long, and it competes with the pygmy shrew (below) as the world's smallest mammal.

Bats

Bats are the only mammals that really fly. Their wings are covered with thin skin. There are two kinds of bats. Small bats feed mainly on night-flying insects. Some also eat fish and frogs.

Fruit bats and flying foxes are large bats with fox-like noses. They live in warm, tropical places, and feed on fruit and the **nectar** of flowers that are open at night.

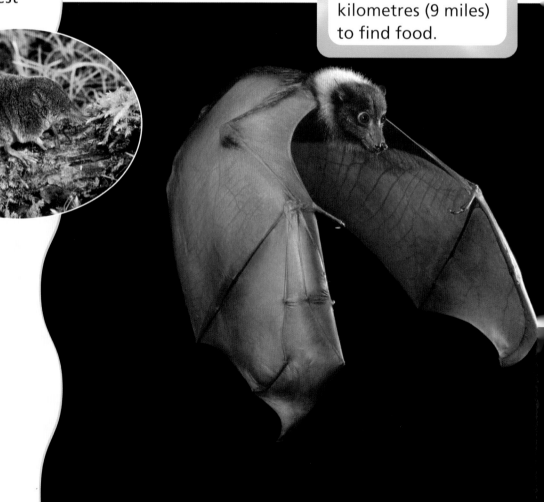

▼ The Indian flying fox will fly up to 14 kilometres (9 miles) to find food.

nectar sugary fluid produced by flowers

Insect-eaters

Shrews, moles, and hedgehogs feed on insects, worms, slugs, and snails. There are about 350 **species** of mammals that eat insects and 960 species of bats. Between them they eat millions of insects every night. They are nature's pest control officers.

The female tenrec can have up to 32 young growing inside her at once. Not all of these will **survive** until birth.

Shrew facts

The American, short-tailed shrew has **venom** in its **saliva**. It uses this to stun insects before it eats them.

▼ The tenrec is a small mammal from Madagascar.

Grass-eaters

Animals that eat only plants are called **herbivores**. More than 200 species of mammals spend most of their time eating grass. Large herbivores, like the rhinoceros, hippopotamus, and elephant, need large amounts of grass and leaves. An elephant can eat 150–300 kilograms (330–660 pounds) in a day.

Zebras, camels, horses, and some other large herbivores have hard toes called hoofs. They also have long legs for running to escape from **predators**.

Heaviest herbivore

The African elephant is the largest living land animal. It weighs 5,400 kilograms (9920 pounds) and can be over 3 metres (10 feet) tall.

▶ This leopard has caught a hare as a snack. It can kill much larger animals.

herbivore animal that eats plants

Meat-eaters

About 300 mammals are **carnivores**. They eat meat or fish. The heaviest is the grizzly bear, which can weigh up to 780 kilograms (1700 pounds).

Many carnivores are hunters and killers. Some, like hyenas, are scavengers. They feed off scraps and **prey** killed by others.

Pandas and some other bears eat only a little meat. Pandas eat bamboo shoots.

Grizzly bears

Grizzly bears hunt alone. In autumn, they may catch salmon as they leap up waterfalls (see below). They also eat insects and fruit.

carnivore animal that eats meat

The biggest mammal

The blue whale is the largest mammal on the planet. Its tail alone is as big as a bus, and can be 7–10 metres (23–32 feet) across.

Sea mammals

Most mammals live on land. But some of the largest and most intelligent mammals live in the sea.

There are 75 **species** of whale, dolphin, and porpoise. Many live in groups called schools. They keep in touch with each other by singing underwater songs that can be heard great distances away.

▲ Bottlenosed dolphins can jump up to 6 metres (20 feet) out of the water.

krill tiny, shrimp-like animals that swim in large numbers in the sea

Feeding

Dolphins and porpoises can go long distances in their search for fish. They work together to round up lots of fish. Then they swim in for the kill.

The massive blue whale can eat more than 40 million **krill** in a day. It feeds by taking in huge gulps of water full of the tiny, shrimp-like krill. It **filters** out the water and swallows the krill.

▼ The bowhead whale can live for 185 years.

blubber layer of fat that protects whales and seals, and keeps them warm

Crowded

Walruses (below) get together at breeding time. They sit themselves tightly on the rocks, so there is hardly room to move.

The male walrus has very long tusks that he can use to protect his females. He may have as many as 50 partners.

Flipper feet

Another group of sea mammals spend some time out of the water. Seals, sealions, and walruses move fast in the sea. Their flippers act like paddles. On land they move slowly, but they need to come on shore to **breed**.

Manatees and dugongs are strange-looking sea mammals. They **graze** on plants in the water and are known as sea cows. The dugong's closest living relative is a land mammal – the elephant.

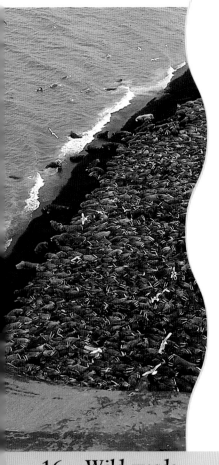

Toothless

Anteaters are the only mammals without any teeth. They flick their long, sticky tongues into ants' nests and lick out hundreds of ants at a time. The giant anteater eats over 10 million ants in a year.

Armadillos, pangolins, and sloths belong to the same mammal group as anteaters. All these animals move slowly, and they all have small teeth, or none at all.

No hurry

It takes a three-toed sloth one minute to move 2 metres (6 feet). Sloths hang upside down in the tops of trees in the South American **rainforest**. They hold on with their claws and eat leaves.

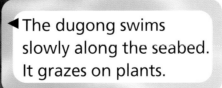

◄ The dugong swims slowly along the seabed. It grazes on plants.

graze feed on plants or grass

Amazing bodies

Fastest

The fastest mammal is the cheetah (below). When it is hunting it can go from 0 to 96 kilometres (60 miles) per hour in under three seconds. That is faster than a Ferrari. It can only keep that speed up for about 500 metres (1650 feet).

Mammals come in many shapes and sizes. Their bodies have **evolved** to fit their different **habitats**.

Swimmers

Many mammals are good swimmers — even those that live inland. Hamsters fill their cheeks with air to help them stay afloat in water. Otters, beavers, and hippos are just as much at home in water as they are on land.

evolve change very slowly over time

Bones and hair

Every mammal has a bony backbone, or spine. The spine gives support for the body. It also protects the nerves that carry messages to and from the brain, and the rest of the body.

The hair, or fur, on mammals helps to keep them at the right temperature. Even humans have tiny hairs all over their bodies. Many mammals grow thicker coats in winter.

Hang glider

A flying squirrel (below) does not actually fly. It **glides** from tree to tree by stretching out its legs. The skin flaps between the legs trap air and act like a hang glider.

◄ Hippos spend most of the day in water. At night they **graze** on land.

Breathing

All mammals breathe in air. The **oxygen** from the air is carried round the body in the blood.

Sea mammals, such as whales and dolphins, need to come to the surface every few minutes to breathe. Seals can dive for about 20 minutes before they need to come up for air. The seal's heart rate slows from 100 beats per minute to only 10 when it is under water. This means it needs less oxygen, so it can stay under the water for longer.

Big-hearted

A giraffe has to have a powerful heart to pump blood all the way up its long neck to its head. Its heart weighs over 11 kilograms (24 pounds) – that is as much as a small dog.

oxygen gas in air and water that all animals and plants need to breathe

Heart rates

The heart rate is the number of times the heart beats in one minute. A tiny mammal like the shrew has a very fast heart rate of 800 beats per minute, even when it is resting. An elephant's heart rate is only 35 beats per minute when it is resting.

The heart pumps blood around the body. A horse's heart pumps about 20 litres (42 pints) of blood every minute. This goes up to 53 litres (112 pints) per minute when the horse starts to gallop.

What is your heart rate?

You need a stopwatch or watch with a second hand to time your heart rate. Sit still and find your **pulse** in your wrist or neck. Count the number of beats in one minute.

▶ A lion's heart rate is 40 when it is resting.

◀ A galloping horse can have a heart rate of up to 250.

pulse heartbeat that can be felt in some places in the body, such as the wrist

Silent songs

Giraffes and elephants look as if they are quietly **grazing** on the African plains. They may be talking over long distances. The sounds they make are too deep for us to hear.

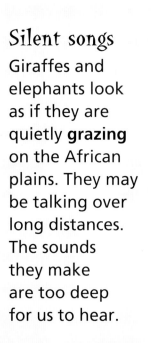

These two European wolves are watching their **prey**.

Senses

Most mammals use their senses of sight, hearing, smell, taste, and touch to help them to find food or a **mate**. Senses also warn of danger. Many mammals have better senses than humans.

   scent trail left by an animal that others can smell and follow

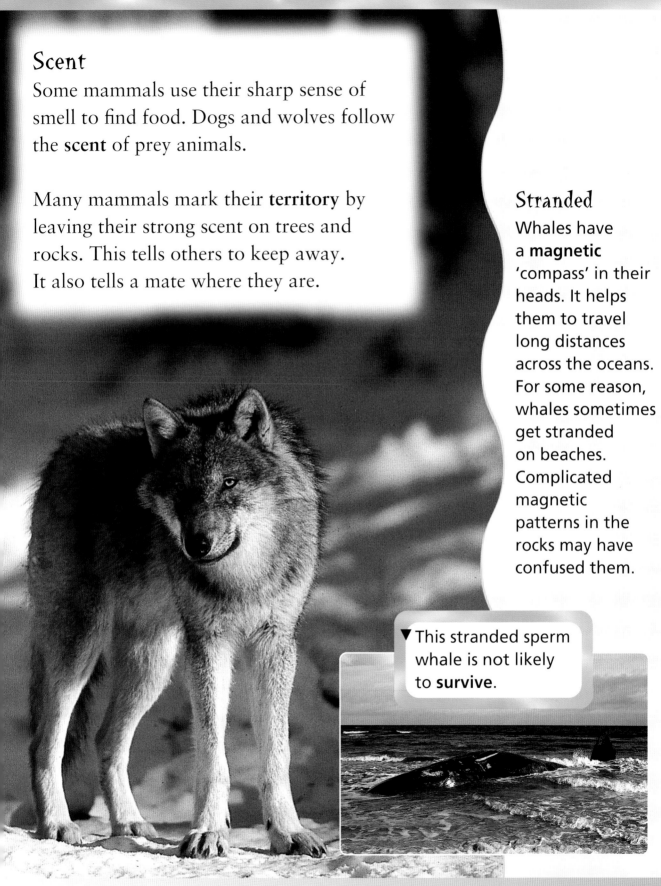

Scent

Some mammals use their sharp sense of smell to find food. Dogs and wolves follow the **scent** of prey animals.

Many mammals mark their **territory** by leaving their strong scent on trees and rocks. This tells others to keep away. It also tells a mate where they are.

Stranded

Whales have a **magnetic** 'compass' in their heads. It helps them to travel long distances across the oceans. For some reason, whales sometimes get stranded on beaches. Complicated magnetic patterns in the rocks may have confused them.

▼ This stranded sperm whale is not likely to **survive**.

magnetic pulling force from the Earth's North and South poles

Feeding

Did you know?

Camels can **survive** for days without food and water. A camel can drink 50 litres (about 90 pints) at one go. Imagine drinking fifty large bottles of water all at once! This keeps the camel going across the desert, until it can find another water hole.

Eating is a full-time job for many mammals. Most of them need to eat often.

Herbivores

All **herbivores** feed on plants. Herbivores that eat mainly grass are called **grazers**. They chew their food for a long time to get all the goodness from it. Many of them graze all day.

Elephants walk several kilometres looking for tree bark, grass, and fruit. They also drink 80 litres (140 pints) of water every day.

▼ Elephants graze for up to 21 hours a day.

Fruit-eaters

Not all herbivores eat grass and leaves. **Primates** such as howler monkeys eat fruit. Tropical bats also live on fruit.

Nibblers

Mice, guinea pigs, and other **rodents** have sharp teeth that are great for nibbling nuts and seeds. These foods are far richer than leaves, so these animals spend less time eating than the grazers.

Stores of fat

Bears and seals have a thick layer of fat that keeps them warm, no matter how cold it is. When food is hard to find, this store of fat also helps to keep them alive.

▲ Howler monkeys eat a lot of fruit.

primate animal that has a large brain, thumbs, and eyes at the front of its head

Pest control

Bats sleep during the day. At sunset they come out to catch mosquitoes and other flies. In one evening, a **colony** of bats can eat half a million flies.

Insect eaters

Insects are a good food for mammals. Shrews, some bats, and anteaters eat nothing else.

Moles, badgers, and skunks all include a few insects and spiders in their diet. So do many **rodents** and monkeys. As moles burrow through the earth, they hunt millipedes, beetles, ants, and worms.

▶ This mole has caught an earthworm.

colony large group of animals living together

Omnivores

A lot of mammals are **omnivores**. This means they eat everything – plants, insects, and meat.

Gorillas are **herbivores**, but many other **primates** are omnivores. They eat small mammals, birds, and eggs. Chimpanzees eat fruit, leaves, monkeys, pigs, and termites. They are the only primates – apart from humans – that hunt in groups.

Vampires

Insects are not enough for South American vampire bats (below). They need about two tablespoons of blood every night. It takes about twenty minutes for the vampire bat to get that much from a horse or cow.

omnivore animal that eats plants and animals

Meat-eaters

Meat-eating mammals are called **carnivores**. They have powerful jaws and sharp, pointed teeth for killing their **prey**.

Hunting takes up a lot of energy. The prey often escapes. Then the carnivore is left hungry and tired. Lions, hyenas, and wolves work together. This way they can hunt larger prey. The whole group then shares the kill.

Pack hunters

Hyenas hunt in packs. These strong animals live in Africa and southern Asia. They have sharp teeth for ripping skin and flesh. As well as catching their own prey, hyenas will eat what is left of another animal's kill.

▼ Lionessess often hunt together to pull down large prey like this buffalo.

prey animal that is killed and eaten by other animals

Big cats

The big cats are fast movers and powerful **predators**. Their sharp teeth and claws help them to attack and kill animals far bigger than themselves.

The most powerful big cat is the tiger. Its striped coat blends with the light and shade of the forest, so it can creep up on its prey.

Man-eaters

Tigers are thought to have killed over one million people during the last 400 years.

When people go into the forest to cut down trees or hunt, they are easy prey for the tiger.

▼ Tigers grab their prey by the throat.

Breeding

Life begins

When mammals mate, the male's **sperm** enters the egg inside the female and **fertilizes** it. The baby mammal now begins to grow inside its mother.

Moose, horses, cattle, and many other **species** of mammal **mate** in the autumn. Their young will be born in the spring. The weather and the good supply of food give the young a chance of **surviving**.

Meeting and mating

When the female is ready to mate, her **scent** changes and the male can tell she is looking for a partner.

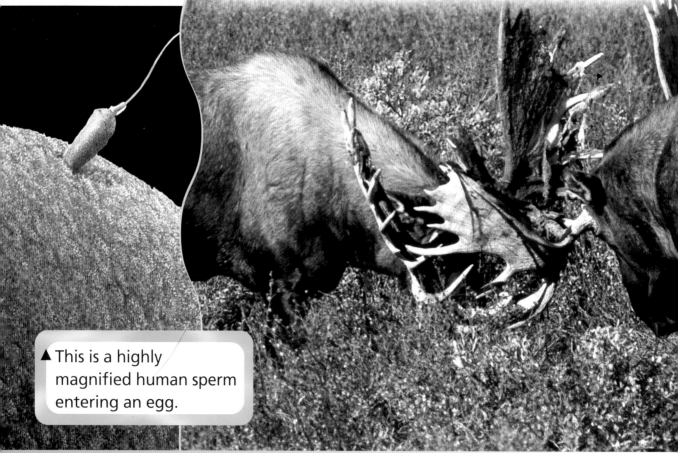

▲ This is a highly magnified human sperm entering an egg.

mate when a male and female come together to produce young

Finding a mate

Male moose travel long distances across North America, looking for a mate. They mark their **territory** and fight other males by locking antlers. The female will mate with the winner. By choosing the strongest male she makes sure her young will be fit and strong.

Male orang-utans call to females across the jungle. They shake branches with a load roar to keep away other males.

▼ Bull moose fight for a mate.

Good timing

Stoats and some other mammals may mate at any time. Even if an egg is fertilized in the summer, it does not grow until the following spring. This is to stop the young stoat being born in the winter. It probably would not survive.

Time to develop

The African elephant is a slow grower. A mother elephant is **pregnant** for two years before giving birth. Mice take only 21 days. Human babies are born after 9 months.

Birth

The baby mammal is fed inside its mother through the **umbilical cord**. The cord connects it to its mother's blood stream. The baby also gets **oxygen** this way. It needs oxygen to breathe.

The mother bites through the cord as soon as the baby is born. It no longer needs the cord. The young mammal can now breathe air for itself. It will be fed with its mother's milk.

umbilical cord cord that joins the baby to its mother while the baby is growing inside her body

Mother bonding

At birth, the mother spends some time licking her newborn clean. While they are so close together, the mother and baby learn each other's **scent**.

This is important for animals that live in large herds, like deer or sheep. They need to be able to find one another.

Baby boom
At only 14 days old, a female lemming can get pregnant. **Lemmings** usually have three **litters** a year. A pair like the ones below once produced 8 litters in less than six months. That is over 100 young.

◄ A mother cleans her newly-born foal. The foal will soon be up on its feet.

Mother's milk

Milk is the mammal's magic. Newborn babies always have liquid food on tap. No other animals have this special way of feeding their young.

The milk is a mixture of water, protein, fats, and vitamins. Each **species** produces milk specially made to meet its needs.

Whale's milk

A baby blue whale (below) drinks over 225 litres (470 pints) of milk a day. All that milk makes it grow fast. It puts on an amazing 4 kilograms (9 pounds) an hour during its first few weeks.

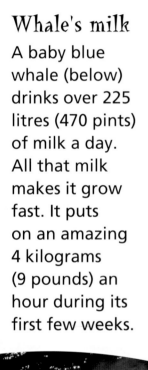

Special milks

Cows, horses, and other **grazing** animals have high-protein milk to make them grow fast and keep up with the herd.

Seal milk is high in fat to help the babies build up a layer of **blubber**. Baby seals keep their fur until they have put on enough blubber to keep them warm in the icy seas. They then grow sleek, adult fur that is better at keeping out water.

▼ A harp seal pup is helpless as it lies in the snow.

Full fat

The baby reindeer (below) is feeding from its mother. Reindeer milk is high in fat. It makes the reindeer calf put on weight fast. This is especially important for mammals that live in the Arctic.

Weird and wonderful

Some mammals need to defend themselves, so that they do not get eaten. A seal pup's white fur makes it nearly invisible against the ice. It is excellent **camouflage**.

Thick-skinned
Three-banded armadillos roll into a ball when a predator comes near (below). Not much can get through its tough skin.

Mammals that are **predators** also need to blend in with their surroundings. The leopard's spots make it hard for others to see it in the shady jungle. Camouflage can help a predator get close to its **prey** without being noticed.

▶ It is possible to smell a skunk from a long way away.

camouflage colours and patterns that match the background

Making a stink

The opossum defends itself by pretending to be dead. It even gives off a smell of dead meat! The attacker will think the opossum is dead and will leave it alone.

Skunks are even smellier. They stamp their feet to warn a predator to back off. If that does not work, the skunk sprays liquid at the attacker's face. The smell is so strong, the attacker can hardly breathe.

▼ This Indian mongoose is attacking a cobra.

Snake-eater

The Indian mongoose eats snakes, even poisonous ones. Over time, it gets used to the **venom**. An older mongoose can even **survive** a cobra bite that would kill a human.

venom poison

Keeping out the cold

Many mammals live in cold places. They have thick fur or **blubber** to help them **survive** in icy places.

The female polar bear digs a den under the snow during the Arctic winter. Her thick fur is made of hollow hairs that trap heat and keep her warm. She gives birth in the den and spends the winter there with her cubs.

Highest

The yak climbs higher than 6000 metres (19,500 feet) in the mountains of Tibet and China. Its long, shaggy coat keeps it warm in the chilly mountains.

▶ Polar bear fur is not really white. The clear hairs reflect light and this makes them look white.

Fur coat

Many mammals grow thicker fur in winter.
A reindeer's winter coat can be 15 centimetres
(6 inches) thick. That is as thick as a mattress!
It helps the reindeer to keep warm at around
30 °C below freezing.

Beavers and otters need to keep warm in cold
water. Their fur is oiled so that water runs off it.
The fur stays dry and traps air next to the skin.
This keeps the otter or beaver warm.

Icy

Whales survive in
freezing water
full of icebergs.
Their thick layers
of blubber keep
them warm.

Using their brains

Mammals are good at thinking and solving problems. They are able to learn new things. Many young mammals grow slowly and are looked after by their parents. This gives them time to play and learn. They find out about their surroundings and they learn by copying their parents and by playing.

Chimpanzees arc quick to learn. Humans have taught some chimpanzees to use signs and grunts so that they can "talk".

Cyber ape

In 1998, a gorilla called Koko was the first non-human to talk using the Internet. Koko had already learnt to use signs, and could put a few words together, such as "more food".

▼ Chimpanzees work out how to use simple tools to get what they want.

Sign language

A chimpanzee called Washoe showed that she could think. She learnt to use more than 100 signs to name different things like "food" and "bird".

One day she saw a swan for the first time, swimming on a lake. Washoe did not know the sign for "swan". She put two signs together and made "water-bird". The people who trained her were amazed.

Clever dolphins

In the wild, dolphins often pick up lumps of sponge and put them on their noses. These protect them from sea snakes as they dig for food. This shows brain power.

▲ These dolphins are learning sign language.

Family life

Marmosets, like the ones below, search for food as a family. They share it – often taking it from each other's mouths. Older brothers and sisters also help with caring for the babies.

Helper

When a female dolphin begins to give birth, she may call another dolphin to help. The **midwife** dolphin helps the mother to push the newborn to the surface. It needs to take its first breath of air straight away. The midwife also helps the mother to protect her young dolphin from sharks for several weeks after it is born.

► Two adult bottlenose dolphins care for a calf.

midwife nurse who helps a mother when she gives birth

Friends and families

Living in families or larger groups makes life easier. There are more eyes on the lookout for danger or food. Parents can share the babysitting with other relatives. The young have playmates to join in their games.

Many mammals seem to need the friendship of others. They also help each other. Vampire bats will bring up some of their meal of blood to share.

Monkey business

Monkeys and baboons **groom** each other. It keeps them clean and is also a way of showing friendship.

groom to keep clean and free of pests

Baby carriers

Kangaroos belong to the small group of **marsupials**. Female marsupials carry their young in **pouches**.

Grey kangaroo **joeys,** or babies, are born after only 4 or 5 weeks. The newborn joey looks like a worm and is only 2.5 centimetres (1 inch) long. It then crawls straight up its mother's belly and into her pouch. The joey quickly begins to feed on the mother's milk.

Laying eggs

The female duck-billed platypus does not give birth to live young. She lays eggs. Platypus babies hatch after ten days and feed on their mother's milk for three or four months.

▶ A large joey still crams itself into its mother's pouch when danger threatens.

▼ The duck-billed platypus lives in and around water in Australia.

marsupial mammal with a pouch for raising its young

Out of the pouch

After 300 days in the pouch, the joey hops out. It carries on drinking its mother's milk for another six months. It still hops back into the pouch whenever it feels afraid.

By 18 months, the joey is getting quite big. It is a bit of a squeeze to get in the pouch. Its legs and tail may stick out. By the time it is fully grown, it will weigh 35,000 times as much as when it was born.

Marsupial facts

- Marsupial comes from the Latin word, *marsupium*, which means "little bag".

- There are 1.5 million kangaroos in Australia.

- A grey kangaroo can jump 13.5 metres (44 feet).

joey baby kangaroo

Migrating

Bison are the largest land mammals in North America. Herds of bison move to new pastures every winter to find better grazing.

On the move

Many herd animals **migrate** to find food. They move to different **grazing** lands at different times of the year.

Wildebeest live in **herds** for safety. It also means there are many mouths to feed. When the dry season comes, there is not enough grass to eat. The wildebeest must set off in search of food. Sometimes they have to cross dangerous rivers to reach good grazing.

▶ A wildebeest herd crosses the Mara River in Kenya, Africa.

migrate travel long distances in search of food or to breed

A million migrate

More than a million wildebeest and 200,000 zebras migrate across the Serengeti Plain in eastern Africa every year. Groups of big cats follow them. The cats **prey on** weak animals that cannot run fast enough to stay with the herd.

Wildebeest calves are able to walk within five minutes of being born. They need to be able to keep up. Their family is always on the move.

Big sleep

You might think that pet cats sleep a lot. On average they are curled up for 13 hours every day. That is nowhere near as much sleep as a koala gets. It spends an amazing 22 hours of each day asleep. Zzzzzzz.

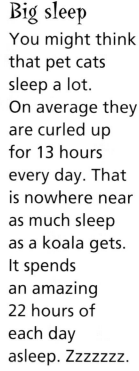

Mammals in danger

On the increase?

The New Zealand southern right whale (below) was thought to be extinct. A few were rediscovered near the Auckland Islands. **Conservationists** are watching them. They hope that their numbers will increase.

About 500 **species** of mammals are in danger of becoming **extinct.** The places where they live are being taken over by people for farming and building. The lives of many mammals are threatened by the destruction of **rainforests.**

In the last 200 years, 30 species of mammals have become extinct. They can never return. This could happen to many more mammals unless people act quickly to protect them.

▶ The giant panda is the symbol for the Worldwide Fund for Nature (WWF), which works to save endangered species.

endangered in danger of dying out

On the brink

Perhaps the best-known **endangered** animal is the giant panda. It lives in the forests in parts of China, where it eats bamboo shoots. Large areas of the forests have been cut down. It is hard for pandas to find food now.

More than 4000 koalas are killed every year in Australia. Their **habitat** is being destroyed. A hundred years ago there were over 3 million koalas. Now there are fewer than 100,000.

Rare rhino

Rhinoceroses have become rare. **Poachers** kill them for their horns. There are fewer than 300 Sumatran rhinos left. They are in danger of disappearing forever.

poacher someone who steals and kills wild animals, although it is against the law

Humans

What are the most dangerous mammals? Humans are the greatest threat to all other mammals. Humans have already made many mammals **extinct**. They have **polluted** and destroyed many places where mammals live. They have also killed many for sport and to make money.

Yet humans may be able to help mammals. Scientists and **conservationists** are working hard to protect **endangered species**.

Messing with nature

Scientists have experimented with **breeding** together different species such as lions and tigers. Their young are called tigons. Cross-breeds are sometimes born deformed and easily get ill. India has stopped all cross-breeding. Hopefully other countries will too.

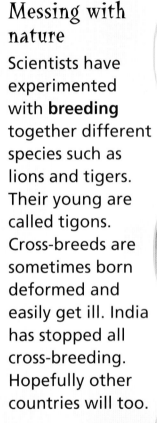

pollution damage caused by chemicals, fumes, and rubbish

Saving gorillas

Lowland gorillas in the forests of central Africa are under threat. Timber companies are cutting down the trees. **Poachers** catch the gorillas and sell them for their meat. In 2001, a disease called ebola killed 80 per cent of the gorillas in Gabon and the Congo.

There is hope for the gorillas. A conservation programme is protecting them with more guards in the national parks.

In the wild

Golden lion tamarins are rare in South America. They were caught and sold as pets. Tamarins have been bred in zoos and put back into the forests. There are now 1200 in the wild.

◄ Lowland gorillas are being returned to the wild.

conservationist someone who protects animals and plants so they do not die out   51

Find out more

Websites

BBC Nature
The 'Wildfacts' website is packed with photos and information about all sorts of animals.
www.bbc.co.uk /nature/animals

Mammal Society
Go to the 'Fun Zone' for quizzes, puzzles, and more. Find out about mammal record breakers.
www.abdn.ac.uk /mammal

Natural History Notebooks
Information and pictures of lots of different mammals.
www.nature.ca /notebooks

Books

Animal Groups, Richard and Louise Spilsbury (Heinemann Library, 2003).
Classifying Living Things: Mammals, Andrew Solway (Heinemann Library, 2003)
From Egg to Adult: The Life Cycle of Mammals, Mike Unwin (Heinemann Library, 2003)
Wild Predators: Wolves and Other Dogs, Andrew Solway (Heinemann Library, 2004)

World wide web

If you want to find out more about mammals you can search the Internet. Use keywords like these:

- "tiger conservation"
- pygmy +shrew
- marsupials

You can find your own keywords by using words from this book. The search tips below will help you find useful websites.

Search tips

There are billions of pages on the Internet. It can be difficult to find exactly what you are looking for. These tips will help you find useful websites more quickly:

- Know what you want to find out about
- Use simple keywords
- Use two to six keywords in a search
- Only use names of people, places, or things
- Put double quote marks around words that go together, for example "tiger conservation"

Where to search

Search engine

A search engine looks through millions of website pages. It lists all the sites that match the words in the search box. You will find the best matches are at the top of the list, on the first page.

Search directory

A person instead of a computer has sorted a search directory. You can search by keyword or subject and browse through the different sites. It is like looking through books on a library shelf.

Answers to 'Can you guess what these are?' on page 4
Largest mammal: blue whale; tallest mammal: giraffe; smallest mammal: pygmy shrew; fastest mammal: cheetah.

Numbers of incredible creatures

Number of species (approximate)

Glossary

blubber layer of fat that protects whales and seals, and keeps them warm

breed to produce young

camouflage colours or patterns that match the background

carnivore animal that eats meat

colony large group of animals living together

conservationist someone who protects animals and plants so they do not die out

endangered in danger of dying out

evolve change very slowly over time

extinct died out, never to return

fertilize when a sperm joins an egg to form a new living thing

filter sift out, or separate, bits from a liquid

glide move smoothly through the air, without flapping

gnaw bite on something hard for a long time, slowly wearing it away

graze feed on plants or grass

groom to keep clean and free of pests

habitat natural home of an animal or plant

herbivore animal that eats plants

herd group of animals

joey baby kangaroo

krill tiny, shrimp-like animals that swim in large numbers in the sea

lemming small rodent, like a hamster

litter group of babies all born to one mother at the same time

magnetic pulling force from the Earth's North and South poles

marsupial mammal with a pouch for raising its young

mate (noun) partner of the opposite sex

mate (verb) when male and female come together to produce young

midwife nurse who helps a mother when she gives birth

migrate travel long distances in search of food or to breed

nectar sugary fluid produced by flowers

omnivore animal that eats plants and animals

oxygen gas in air and water that all animals and plants need to breathe

poacher someone who steals and kills wild animals, although it is against the law

pollute to make air, water, or land dirty or dangerous

pollution damage caused by chemicals, fumes, and rubbish

pouch pocket in which marsupials carry their babies

predator animal that kills and eats other animals

pregnant expecting a baby or babies

prey animal that is killed and eaten by other animals

prey on live by hunting and eating other animals

primate animal that has a large brain, thumbs, and eyes at the front of its head

pulse heartbeat that can be felt in some places in the body, such as the wrist

rainforest dense forest in tropical region

rodent animal with gnawing teeth that keep on growing throughout its life

saliva juices made by the mouth to help chewing and digestion

scent trail left by an animal that others can smell and follow

species type of animal or plant

sperm male sex cell

survive stay alive despite danger and difficulties

territory area defended by a particular animal

umbilical cord cord that joins the baby to its mother while the baby is growing inside her body

venom poison

vertebrate animal that has a backbone

Index

Titles in the *Freestyle Express*: *Incredible Creatures* series include:

Hardback: 1844 434516

Hardback: 1844 434524

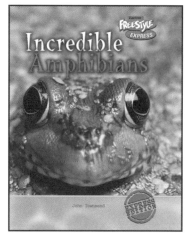

Hardback: 1844 434532

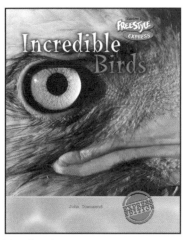

Hardback: 1844 434540

Hardback: 1844 434761

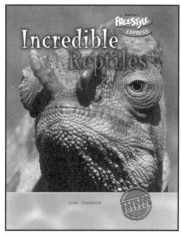

Hardback: 1844 43477X

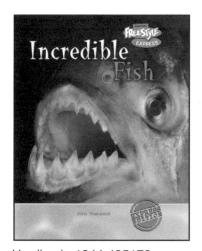

Hardback: 1844 435172

Hardback: 1844 435180

Find out about other Freestyle Express titles on our website www.raintreepublishers.co.uk